To Richard Bailey
for the gift of confidence.

from desolation.
ashes.
a little flower
emerges.

By Criscelda Mortimore

from desolation. ashes. a little flower emerges.
All rights reserved.
Printed in the United States of America.
2018, second edition 2020

Book cover designed by ZevsPrime.
ISBN 978-1-7356289-0-5

Table of Contents

all of the old
encrusted upon me
must
harden
crack
and fall off.

My Mother's Mouth	2
Two Sisters	3
Not Invited In	4
The Working Poor	5
Nothing	6
Escape	7
Obedience	8

The Unicorn
has gone insane
and The Rose
has been trampled.

A Man's New Mother	10
Mutual Use	11
Father of David, My Most Beautiful	12

Into the strained-neck
despair
God sends
a tiny
blue
sea turtle.

Window	14
The Cult of Motherhood	15
Martha	16
Moth	17
Motherly Intercession	18

I pray for a little candle to hold with me
in this dark and empty space within.

Cleveland	20
Farewell, My Child	23
Knife	25
Your Smile	26
For My Beautiful Friend	28
Recidivism	29
Crater	30
On Their Heads	31

A therapist:
One
who sits
with you
in the isolated
room.

Creature of the Dark	34
Dream Brother	35
On Therapy	36
Ascending	37
Splinter	38
But First We Dance	39
In My Hightower	40
Sullen Girl	41
Forgiveness	42
Silent and Green	43
Creature of Ezekiel	44

Hope
invades
where it has
no right to be.

Sven	46
Filled With Pleasure	47
Something Special	48
Strange	49
Black, White and Blue	50
Warriors of Beauty	51
I'm a Poet	52
Faith	53

IV

all of the old
encrusted upon me
must
harden
crack
and fall off.

My Mothers Mouth

My mother's mouth
is filled
with sharp teeth.

Her jaws
snap!
and surprise me
every time.

A mother
can't be
a terrible beast
can she?

Two Sisters

Two sisters, two completely different ways
to deal with heavy, unexpected blows
the younger one would make the dealer pay
the older one would curl up and lie low.

One day a clash began between the brute
and the small young one, not afraid to fight
the clash became a battle absolute
the young one kept herself safe with a bite.

But soon the brawl became a scary sound
with smashing, slamming rising up nonstop
the older sister feared the fiend would pound
the younger one and so she called the cops.

The bully attacks, angry and obese
You traitor! How dare you call the police!

Not Invited In

A family man commits a heinous deed
horrific, what's behind that friendly face
betrayal, lust, deception, selfish greed
fair swine, upheld, protected from disgrace.

Who ought to be condemned in this grim scene?
A girl is forced to spend time with her kin
he drugs to spread her legs and go between
his wife, also receives a Mickey Finn.

The wife, "asleep," is lying on the rug
the girl, thought safe, is lying on the couch
he violates, his acts met with a shrug
the blameless girl receives all the fallout.

And although she did not commit the sin
she's outside, shamed, and not invited in.

The Working Poor

My mother had a strange way to instruct
whene'er I acted up she threw me out.
To pay my rent I started cleaning muck
a janitor, eighteen-years old, without.

Without an education or a skill
I found myself surrounded by adults
the working poor, existence wished them ill
their day-to-day subsistence difficult.

I learned that all are treated with respect
ha ha, just kidding, just the opposite
despite our toil, our poverty abject
more skillful workers treated us like shit.

A brazen joy, though shamed, they did impart
and to them I'll always incline my heart.

Nothing

There is nothing
so difficult to wrestle with
than nothing

There is nothing
so completely warped
as that which had the potential
to be completely perfect

A mother
can become a demon
impossible to detangle
impossible to know
impossible to escape

a sweet night of perfect, effortless rest
becomes a night of endless torture
as your mind
wrestles with nothing
fighting
fighting
and dragging
your poor helpless body
along with it.

Escape

The curse
it has not shattered me yet.

I love to laugh
and I love to forget.

And as for forgetting
the lurking thing

I love to dance
even more
to sing.

I love to think on
the lovely and fair
and as for the ugly
I have only my prayer

"Lord bless me and keep me
always be with me
and keep me safe from the monster."

Obedience

A dog
sits
with his owner
a homeless
man.

It is raining
it is cold

the cold
wet
concrete
causes the dog
discomfort.

The dog
tries
to avoid
touching
the ground
with his haunches.

The man
yells at the dog
"sit!"
The dog
sits.

The Unicorn
has gone insane
and The Rose
has been trampled.

A Man's New Mother

A wife
is a man's new mother
from one breast to another
from a mother's cradling
arms
to a wife's
cradling legs
new hands
to rub your back
to sleep
and to buy you
long underwear
and deliver them…with a kiss.

Mutual Use

Take this ring
with it
I lasso you.
You
are my hole
to fill.

Take this ring
with it
I satisfy myself.
You
are to fulfill me.

Father of David, My Most Beautiful

Father of David
my most beautiful

I wish you were
a tall glass
of cool clear water
so that I could drink you down.

I wish you were
a snug bed
so that I could climb inside you
and pull your covers over me.

I wish you were
a tiny baby
so that I could cradle
all of you
in my arms.

Father of David
my most beautiful.

Into the strained-neck
despair
God sends
a tiny
blue
sea turtle.

Window

The branches and the shadows did conspire
seraphic face upon the window pane
I did believe it was a signal fire
that image I would need it to sustain
my will as I began to journey t'ward
that enclosed city bustling in my midst
although I only knew her as abhorred
and everyone I looked to did forbid'st
that I should ever see her being more
that satan's greatest swindle and deceit
a most polluted babylonic whore
who over time more trappings did accrete
but now that I have come to live inside
a window I shall be in the divide.

The Cult of Motherhood

Hold the standard
so high
that all of our flaws
are exaggerated.

Edit yourself
until
your outward presentation
is a lie.

Tie up heavy burdens
and lay them on our shoulders
while whispering in our ears
"resting
is wrong."

So deep
is our love
Without end
our concern
So open
our hearts
that it is easy
to reach in
grip our souls

and squeeze.

Martha

The cancer from your vigor made you fall.
Self-conscious as you would adjust your wig.
Easy to break as you would snap a twig.
My eyes upon you, I began to bawl.

The love I had received it had been small.
The love you had for me it was so big.
I lapped it up, fulfilled from my first swig.
The way you made me feel I still recall.

Giver of love you were the only one.
Your humble home provided me relief.
'Twas poor and small and everything
  homespun.
'Tis empty now and fills me with such grief.

My time with you had only just begun.
This love I got to have it was so brief.

Moth

Brown.
Plain.
Strange.
She will burn herself
in her single-minded
enslaving
love
for the light.

Weak.
Small.
Frail.
You could damage
her wings
with your fingertips.

Yet.
She can still go
undetected
to the towers
in the dark places.

Rest on my sleeve
strange
little
brown
moth.

Motherly Intercession

A child developing within my womb
without, my little girl she dallies, calm
the centipede he eavesdrops in the room
he caught my eye, of horror I felt a qualm.

Disgusting, with his many filthy legs
all held together by a giant piece
'twas still a moment, then t'ward us he sped
unmitigated evil spirit unleashed.

His legs behaving like a hover board
a kamikaze purpose to destroy
his head erect, he flew across the floor
my massive sneakers; stout legs I deployed

and underneath my shoe, complete the crush
a great mass of bent legs and twitching mush.

I pray for a little candle
 to hold with me
in this dark and empty
 space within.

Cleveland

I'm so glad it's raining.
It's like Cleveland
knows how I feel.
It's like my sorrow
billowed out of me
and into the atmosphere.

I give up.
I put down my cross.
It truly is a cross
It truly leaves me powerless.
All I want
is escape.

Cleveland
You know how I feel
Cleveland
Cry with me
Cry for me.

How could anyone?
Really count the cost?

Jesus, your path
is horrible
Why would anyone choose it?

It does not pay
to do what is right.

In fact,
it costs extra.
Much extra.

It is no wonder then
That most people
choose
to cut corners
Slide by.
Look the other way.

Why pay to work hard
When you can keep a false sense of peace
at such low cost?

For though it is false
It feels kind.
It feels like a smile.
It feels light.
It feels like freedom.
It feels like happiness.

I want those feelings.
Even if they are false.
Even if others have to suffer
so that I may have them.

Others
care not
if I should suffer.
Why should I care?
Why not join the crowd?

I could stop struggling then
Let the current of the crowds
carry me.

For though the stream
may be filthy
at least
I will be carried.
Instead of having to carry
the filth of others.
Waiting.
Hoping.
That one day they may be clean.

Farewell, My Child

I stand here
at this unmarked grave
a single tear
falls down my cheek
for the girl
who has died.

It was a long, slow death.
She screamed.
She cried and cried for help.
But her savior did not care.
She lay in disbelief.
She gave up.

Farewell, my child.
Gone are your foolish beliefs,
Gone are your beautiful delusions,
Gone is your false hope.

The ground
in your secret garden
broke beneath you
and swallowed you whole.

Goodbye, dear child.
I will always miss you.
For though you were foolish,
you were warm.
And all I have now
is cold, lonely reason.

Knife

Your gunmetal sheen
your weight
pressing against my palm
slicing through
a
red
ripe
tomato.

Your Smile

Your smile
is like
an explosion of stars.
Bursting forth
Daring
Perfectly unaware
that you don't belong
in this world
of blood
and limbs
and sadness
and darkness.

I despair
at the weight
of the carnage.

I crumble
upon hearing
the wolves
of fear.

But your smile
what light!
Such beauty
does not belong
here.

And yet
I am so grateful
that it is.

For My Beautiful Friend

Beautiful.
You are.
It has
nothing to do
with your features
with your body.
Your beauty
hides.
One must
pass the hours
with you
to see it.
But when they do
it rises
like a tall man
revealing himself
after crouching
in the shadows.

Recidivism

I've come
to love
my golden dungeon.

I spin around
on it's shiny floors.
I fear
that, should I ever leave
I would be
arrested
a few weeks later.

And tears
of joy
would stream
down my face
as they dragged me back
to that familiar place.

Crater

I can see
the crater.
I know
that I am always
trying
to fill it
to numb the ache
of it's presence.
I know that I
am not
the only one.
Any fixation
a false remedy.
In the end
you will become
a crater
too.

On Their Heads

My dream
is to be
nothing.

My dream
is to be
rejected.

My wish
is to fall apart.

All of my dreams
have come true.

A therapist:
One
who sits
with you
in the isolated
room.

Creature of the Dark

My faith has led to places unforeseen
each time that you see me I'm someone new.
Escaped – the gargoyle; dragon sly, unseen
the fowler's snare torn, and away I flew.

My mind knows that that time is over now
it happened oh so many years ago
I've crammed three lifetimes into one somehow
enough to realize how much I don't know.

There is a force, a torment which doth twist
the souls of people and it leaves them warped
the child I was has now ceased to exist
the past I cling to, nothing but a corpse

but still, the things that harm have left their mark
and so, I reach, a creature of the dark.

Dream Brother

What is wrong?
with soldiering on?
Why do you insist
that I stop
and feel?

What is wrong?
With keeping my demons?
Locked in an abyss
Why do you insist
that I release them?

I set one free
you saw what it did to me.
My fear is not unwarranted.

Dream Brother.
Hold my hand.
I will face these monsters
if you come with me.

On Therapy

I told you
not to open
those
Pandora's Boxes
Now the imps
are running free
up to
all kind
of trickery.

Ascending

Drifting
over
my planet
in
my
hot air balloon.

I see
my heart
on the ground
smashed
destroyed
like roadkill.

A tear
rolls
down my cheek.

I increase
the flame
and ascend.

Splinter

I pulled
a splinter
the size
of a sapling
from
my heart.

And now
I feel
much better.

But First We Dance

Why can't I just pretend?
To be happy?
Fake it 'till you make it.
'Till you make it
out the window.

Why can't I just whistle?
As I work?
Alongside the crater?
Taking a cigarette smoke break
as though it were no big deal?

It's not going away.
Talking about it won't make it go away.
Thinking about it won't make it go away.
Analyzing it won't make it go away.
Why not dance?
Before hurling yourself?
Into the pit?

In My Hightower

In my hightower
where I've gone
to die.

There are still
pleasures
to be had.

Sometimes
I look
out the window.

The birds
fly by
in droves
wild
yet orchestrated
droves.

Up here
they make me smile
in a way
that, they never could
when
I was on
the ground.

Sullen Girl

The peaceful waters grow tumultuous
discouraged, I begin to spiral down
events, unmanaged, pile calamitous
each small disturbance hurls me t'ward
  meltdown.

Obsessions, they are eating me alive
they carry me away, army of ants
above me, black clouds I cannot survive
swirling tornado, storm vociferant.

I look for You, I'm totally unmoored
I finally find You, blissfully asleep
my situations, I've in full absorbed
what contrast to that baffling calm you keep!

I gaze at You and think it would behoove
my soul to cling to You and thus be soothed.

Forgiveness

For making me feel worthless
I forgive you.

For forcing me to lessen myself
I forgive you.

For always siding with my oppressors
I forgive you.

For refusing to listen to me
I forgive you.

I let it all
drop
into the abyss
as if
it never was.

Silent and Green

It's silent
and green.

The chaos
swirls
outward
and away.

The chaos
falls
backward
and off.

I emerge
pink
and new.

Creature of Ezekiel

I am slowly
coming out
of my cocoon.

All those
who knew me
as a caterpillar
are shaken
unsettled.

But this
is me.

I'm sorry
for having disturbed you
but now
it is time
to fly.

Hope
invades
where it has
no right to be.

Sven

An angel
came to me.

He was old
his body
sagged
his nose
was rotting.

But his eyes!
a piercing blue.
Piercing through
the membrane
from the other
dimension.

He stood
quietly
calmly
and told me
what I ought to do.

Then he
departed
from my
heart.

And my heart
reaches out
for him
still.

Filled With Pleasure

Pour wine
into my mouth.

My wet mouth
filled with pleasure.

Something Special

The words
I have
with you
are heavy.

They send
pieces
gliding
with
a mere
tap.

Strange

I always was considered to be strange
and have worked hard to pass as one of them
regarding social skills, I was shortchanged
for being very much I was condemned.

I've been told that I am too sensitive
and also that my head is in the clouds
emotional and too inquisitive
with over-active fancies I'm endowed.

Although these qualities rejection brought
they serve me very well in poetry
the beauty others miss, easy to spot
in strawberries and avocado seeds.

And so, no longer will I spurn my fate
I'm strange and into it I'll lean my weight.

Black, White and Blue

Hands
full of blueberries
black
white
and blue.

Crush them
in my hands
let the juice
slide down
my wrists.

Warriors of Beauty

I feel a kinship with the honeybees.
They leave their hive to find what's beautiful
they take the nectar from what's blossoming
store it away, alchemic miracle.

And artists, too, must leave what they find safe
and even in great sadness find what's good
they must endure, no matter how it chafes
then give forth honey once they have withstood.

But honeybees are not only what's sweet
and beauty has it's painful counterpart
their stinger, once used, renders obsolete
the tiny bee by tearing it apart.

Be blessed, warriors of beauty who impart
the sweetness and brutality of art.

I'm a Poet

I'm a poet.
I wear
wrinkled clothing.

I'm a poet.
If I love you
I
Love
You.

I'm a poet
When I speak
my words
fall
awkwardly
out of my mouth
and strike the floor
like
clamshells.

But
give me a pencil
a sharp pencil
and you will know
how I feel.

Faith

Please know
that contrary
to evidence
you are loved.

My prayer
for you
is that
this love
may break through
in a sigh
in a compassionate look
in someone's eye.

For love
is a miraculous thing
Even if scantly given
such a small seed
can grow
into a powerful tree
whose branches
reach forth
and embrace

Love
flowering into the world
it's fragrance
healing the stench.

The End

www.ingramcontent.com/pod-product-compliance
Lightning Source LLC
Chambersburg PA
CBHW020914080526
44589CB00011B/597